THE STORY OF THE
KANSAS CITY CHIEFS

NFL TODAY

THE STORY OF THE KANSAS CITY CHIEFS

SCOTT CAFFREY

CREATIVE EDUCATION

Cover: Chiefs defense, 1967 (top), tight end Tony
Gonzalez (bottom)
Page 2: Wide receiver Dwayne Bowe
Pages 4–5: Coach Hank Stram (left) and linebacker
Willie Lanier (right)
Pages 6–7: Chiefs offense, 1969

....

Published by Creative Education
P.O. Box 227, Mankato, Minnesota 56002
Creative Education is an imprint of
The Creative Company
www.thecreativecompany.us

Design and production by Blue Design
Design Associate: Sarah Yakawonis
Printed in the United States of America

Photographs by Getty Images (Vernon Biever/
NFL, Rich Clarkson/Sports Illustrated, Jonathan
Daniel, Stephen Dunn, James Flores/NFL, Focus
On Sport, George Gojkovich, Rod Hanna/NFL, Tom
Hauck, Jeff Haynes/AFP, Andy Hayt, Walter Iooss
Jr./Sports Illustrated, Dave Kaup/AFP, David E.
Klutho/Sports Illustrated, G. Newman Lowrance,
Al Messerschmidt, NFL Photos, Darryl Norenberg/
NFL, Panoramic Images, Jamie Squire, Rick Stewart,
Barry Taylor/MLS, Al Tielemans/Sports Illustrated,
Tim Umphrey, Ron Vesely)

Library of Congress Cataloging-in-Publication Data

Caffrey, Scott.
The story of the Kansas City Chiefs / by Scott
Caffrey.
p. cm. — (NFL today)
Includes index.
ISBN 978-1-58341-760-7
1. Kansas City Chiefs (Football team)—History—
Juvenile literature. I. Title. II. Series.

GV956.K35C35 2009
796.332'6409778411—dc22   2008022692

First Edition
9 8 7 6 5 4 3 2 1

CONTENTS

ON THE SIDELINES

MEET THE CHIEFS

FROM TEXANS TO CHIEFS

X

There are two Kansas Cities in the central United States, separated by the Missouri River. Kansas City, Missouri, is located along the eastern edge of the river, while Kansas City, Kansas, is at the western edge. Founded in 1838, Kansas City, Missouri, is the larger of the neighboring "twin" cities. "K.C." is heralded for its contributions to jazz and blues music and has become famous for its unique style of barbecue. And since 1963, it has been home to a beloved football team called the Chiefs.

The Chiefs' story began not in Missouri but in Texas. In 1959, Texas millionaire Lamar Hunt established the American Football League (AFL) after having been repeatedly turned down by the National Football League (NFL) in his requests to start a new franchise in Dallas, Texas. He gathered seven other millionaire peers to become team owners, and the AFL began competing directly with the NFL. "It was an era when the game of pro football was really ready to grow," Hunt said. "Also, the United States had a lot of markets that didn't have pro football."

Hunt was so confident that pro football would succeed in Dallas that he named his club the Texans, after a team that had previously failed there in 1952. Hunt stocked his roster with local talent to generate fan interest. One of these

X More than 170 years after its founding, Kansas City is today a scenic middle-American metropolis nicknamed "The City of Fountains" due to its more than 200 water fountains.

players was speedy running back Abner Haynes of North Texas State University. In 1960, Haynes would establish himself as the AFL's first star, leading the league in rushing attempts (156), yards (875), and touchdowns (9) and capturing Player of the Year honors.

Hank Stram, a little-known assistant coach at the University of Miami, was hired in 1960 as the team's first head coach. "I met Hank and was impressed," Hunt later said. "He had that good reputation of having an offensive mind, and gosh, he was ready to do it." Stram would go on to coach the team for 15 seasons, develop many offensive and defensive innovations, and lead the franchise to some of its greatest moments.

In 1960, the NFL created the Dallas Cowboys franchise to compete against the Texans. As the Texans went a middling 14–14 over the course of their first two seasons, they had trouble drawing fans. In 1962, they added little-used NFL quarterback Len Dawson, a player Stram remembered from his time as an assistant coach at Purdue University. After floundering between the Pittsburgh Steelers and the Cleveland Browns, Dawson's confidence had waned, and his skills had eroded. But Stram argued that Dawson was a great quarterback who just needed a fresh start.

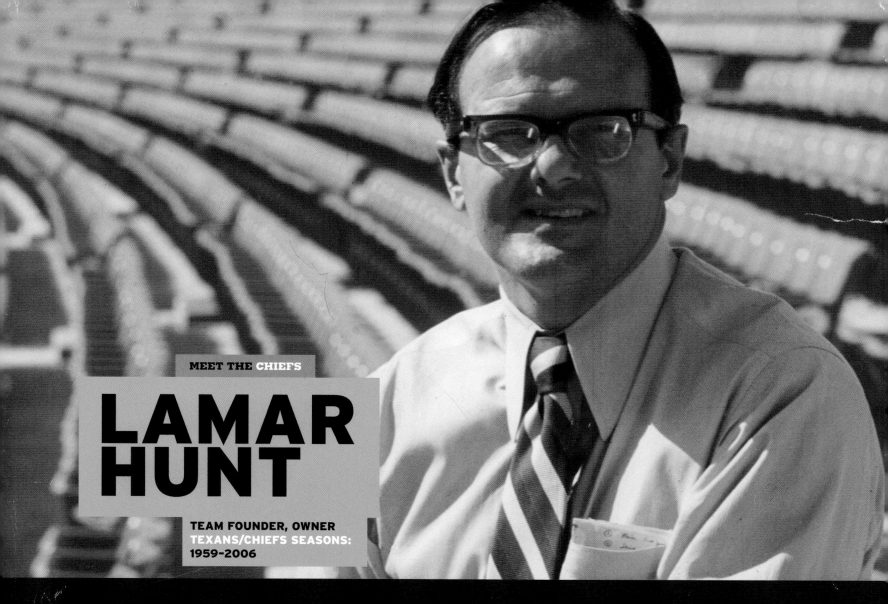

LAMAR HUNT

**TEAM FOUNDER, OWNER
TEXANS/CHIEFS SEASONS:
1959-2006**

Lamar Hunt earned the nickname "Games" for being a huge sports fan when he was a reserve tight end on the Southern Methodist University football team. After founding the Texans (who became the Chiefs) and spearheading the AFL, Hunt extended his reach far beyond football with the creation of a tennis league (World Championship Tennis) and team ownership in basketball (the National Basketball Association's Chicago Bulls) and minor league baseball (the Dallas-Fort Worth Spurs). But among his biggest achievements was jump-starting the "other football" in America with the North American Soccer League (NASL) in 1967. He owned the Dallas Tornado franchise, which went on to win the NASL championship in 1971. After the NASL discontinued its operations, Hunt kept his ownership hand in soccer through three Major League Soccer teams: the Kansas City Wizards, Columbus Crew, and FC Dallas. A member of many different sports halls of fame, Hunt was the first AFL member inducted into the Pro Football Hall of Fame in 1972. "He loved sports so much," his wife Norma said. "He was so passionate about them, and he wanted others to share the joy."

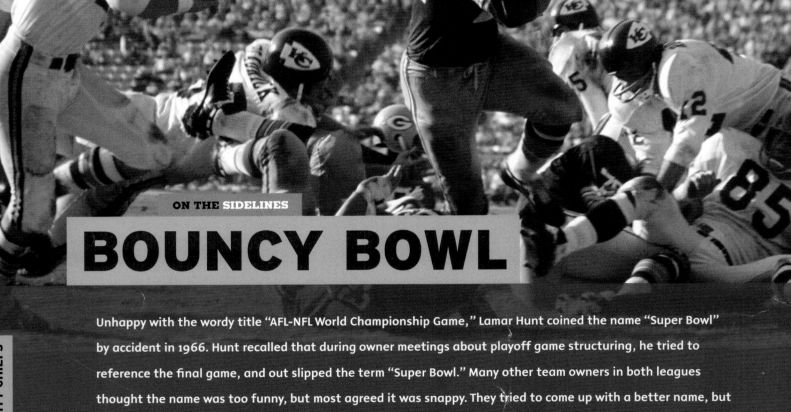

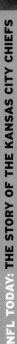
ON THE SIDELINES

BOUNCY BOWL

Unhappy with the wordy title "AFL-NFL World Championship Game," Lamar Hunt coined the name "Super Bowl" by accident in 1966. Hunt recalled that during owner meetings about playoff game structuring, he tried to reference the final game, and out slipped the term "Super Bowl." Many other team owners in both leagues thought the name was too funny, but most agreed it was snappy. They tried to come up with a better name, but no one could, and so it stuck. "My own feeling is that it probably registered in my head because my daughter, Sharron, and my son, Lamar Jr., had a children's toy called a Super Ball," Hunt explained, "and I probably interchanged the phonetics of 'bowl' and 'ball.'" After two years, Hunt's "Super Bowl" became the name of the game. That year, in a note to NFL commissioner Pete Rozelle, Hunt suggested adding roman numerals to give the game "more dignity." So, after the third Super Bowl, roman numerals were grandfathered in and added to the first trio of games. And the Super Bowl as we know it was named forever.

Stram's gamble was a triumph. In 1962, Dawson led the surprising Texans to the AFL Western Division title and the AFL Championship Game. Dawson emerged as a star as he led the AFL in completion percentage and tossed a league-high 29 touchdowns. "There is no passer in professional football more accurate than Lenny," Stram said.

Dawson didn't do it all by himself, though. Haynes scored a league-record 19 touchdowns to go along with 1,622 total yards, while linebacker Sherrill Headrick and cornerback Dave Grayson spearheaded a fierce defense. In the 1962 AFL Championship Game, these players carried the Texans to a 20–17 overtime victory over their intrastate rivals, the Houston Oilers.

Despite the Texans' championship, Hunt had decided that Dallas wasn't big enough for two teams, and he relocated

X Although a bit undersized for a professional quarterback, Len Dawson made up for it with his unflappable poise and precise passing.

A member of the original Texans roster in 1960, linebacker Sherrill Headrick seemed impervious to pain, playing through many injuries. **X**

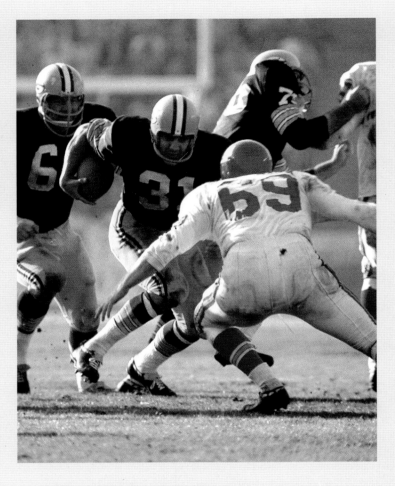

his club to Kansas City before the start of the 1963 season. General manager Jack Steadman convinced Hunt that the proud American Indian moniker "Chiefs" was more suitable to represent the Missouri city, and the Kansas City Chiefs were born. Although the great play of Dawson and Haynes quickly won over new fans in the "Show Me State," the Chiefs were a mediocre team in their first two seasons there, going 5–7–2 and 7–7.

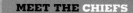

HANK STRAM

COACH
TEXANS/CHIEFS SEASONS: 1960-74

During the decade-long history of the AFL, Hank Stram won more games and more league championships (1962, 1966, 1969) than any other coach and was the only coach in the AFL's history to take his team to two Super Bowls, winning one. Stram was known for his creative innovations. On offense, he developed the "moving pocket," which took advantage of quarterback Len Dawson's scrambling ability. He also devised the "two-tight-end" alignment, which provided an extra blocker and helped slow down the opposition's pass rush. On defense, he created the "stack defense." This positioned the linebackers behind the defensive linemen, allowing the linebackers to react more quickly to the opposing offense. He also always used a nose tackle across from center. These innovations helped Stram mine the most out of his players' talents. Willie Lanier, Bobby Bell, and Jim Lynch were considered by many to be the best linebacker trio in the AFL. By 2008, Stram and five of his Chiefs players— Dawson, Lanier, Bell, Buck Buchanan, and Jan Stenerud—were enshrined in the Pro Football Hall of Fame.

K.C. ON THE
WARPATH

In 1965, the Chiefs bolstered their offense by drafting Otis Taylor, a receiver with the complete package of size, speed, strength, and agility. Taylor also had confidence. "I'll tell you something about Otis Taylor," he said of himself. "He wants to be the best—always. There hasn't been a year when he didn't want to score more touchdowns than anybody and gain more yardage than anybody. At the start of the season, I aim for the top 10 and higher. And I don't quit."

In 1966, powerful linebackers Bobby Bell and E. J. Holub helped the Chiefs win the Western Division and pound the Buffalo Bills 31–7 in the AFL Championship Game to bring home the franchise's second league title. In previous seasons, that would have been the ultimate accomplishment. But the AFL had established itself as a major sports attraction, and its champion was set to take on the NFL's champion in the first Super Bowl to determine a true world champion. The Chiefs faced the Green Bay Packers and their legendary coach, Vince Lombardi, in Super Bowl I.

The heavily favored Packers scored first. Although the Chiefs struggled offensively, Dawson tied the game in the second quarter with a touchdown pass to dependable fullback Curtis McClinton. But the Packers and their star quarterback, Bart Starr, proved too powerful for the young

X Stretching the field with an average of more than 22 yards a catch in 1966, big receiver Otis Taylor also posted the AFL's longest touchdown catch that season, an 89-yard score.

Chiefs and pulled away in the second half to win 35–10.

After going 9–5 in 1967, Kansas City improved to 12–2 in 1968 and tied for first in the Western Division with their archrivals, the Oakland Raiders, who soundly beat the Chiefs 41–6 in the playoffs. Undaunted by the ouster, Kansas City came back stronger than ever in 1969 behind a hard-hitting defense that featured star linebacker Willie Lanier and bruising tackle Junious "Buck" Buchanan. After narrowly beating the New York Jets 13–6 in the playoffs, the Chiefs dispatched Oakland 17–7 in the championship game—the final game in AFL history. With tremendous momentum, they made a triumphant return to the Super Bowl, where they met the Minnesota Vikings.

Most football fans expected the Vikings to win Super Bowl IV. But kicker Jan Stenerud booted three field goals to give Kansas City an early 9–0 lead. After the Chiefs recovered a fumbled Vikings kickoff, running back Mike Garrett plunged in for a touchdown. Safety Johnny Robinson stood out by playing with three broken ribs to ring up two interceptions and a fumble recovery as the defense obliterated Minnesota's offense.

With the score 16–7 in the third quarter, Dawson hit Taylor with a short pass and watched the star receiver high-step

Willie Lanier was not only the heart of the Chiefs defense but a pro football pioneer—the first black player to star at middle linebacker.

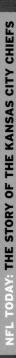

STRAM ON RECORD

Today, the NFL Films studio commonly uses portable microphones to put television viewers within earshot of the on-field action. Many coaches, players, and officials have been asked to wear microphones over the years. But the first such request went to Hank Stram, one of football's most colorful characters, in Super Bowl IV after the 1969 season. And in the process, NFL Films captured an in-depth look at a good-natured coach winning the game of his life. Viewers got to watch and hear Stram as he energetically coached and quipped all game long. He posed one of the most common coach-to-official questions in the history of sports: "How in the world can all six of you miss a play like that?" But perhaps the most fascinating moment was his prediction that the play "Sixty-five Toss Power Trap" to running back Mike Garrett would break for a touchdown. The recorded spotlight served Stram well after his coaching tenure ended. He spent 17 years calling Monday Night Football games on the radio alongside legendary broadcaster Jack Buck. His trademark was his ability to accurately predict the next play.

for a 46-yard touchdown, sealing a 23–7 Chiefs victory. "Our game plan wasn't very complicated," said Dawson, who was named Super Bowl Most Valuable Player (MVP). "It involved throwing a lot of formations at them—formations they hadn't seen during the course of the season."

In 1970, when the AFL merged with the NFL, the Chiefs slipped to 7–5–2. But in 1971, they met the Miami Dolphins in an epic, double-overtime playoff game. The usually reliable Stenerud missed a field goal as regulation time expired, then missed another game-winning opportunity in overtime. Finally, the Dolphins' Garo Yepremian kicked a field goal in the second overtime to hand the Chiefs a heartbreaking 27–24 loss. The 82-minute and 40-second marathon still stands as the longest contest in NFL history.

Despite some great performances by scrappy halfback Ed Podolak, Coach Stram's squad then slid out of contention. A move into the new Arrowhead Stadium in 1972 provided some excitement, but the team continued to struggle. Still, faithful Chiefs fans showed up to cheer for such Pro-Bowlers as cornerback Emmitt Thomas and nose tackle Curley Culp.

LEAN YEARS AT ARROWHEAD

Hank Stram was fired after the 1974 season, Dawson and Taylor both retired in 1975, and the Chiefs slipped into the bottom half of the American Football Conference (AFC) West Division. "Our downfall was because of a mistake I made in the early '70s," Lamar Hunt later recalled. "Hank wanted to run the whole operation … but it was too much for one man to handle. I made a mistake of letting him tend in that direction. There was a period where we didn't do a good enough job of scouting. We didn't do a good enough job of bringing in players."

Even as new heroes emerged, including hard-hitting defensive end Art Still, losing became a habit in Kansas City. Paul Wiggin, Stram's successor, oversaw back-to-back 5–9 seasons. Then, in 1977, after the team started 1–6, Hunt fired Wiggin in midseason, and the Chiefs finished with a franchise-worst 2–12 record.

Under new coach Marv Levy, the Chiefs climbed to a respectable 8–8 in 1980. The team's future looked bright when it drafted running back Joe Delaney in 1981. At

Although often overshadowed by the great Willie Lanier, Jim Lynch (pictured) was a terrific linebacker in his own right, roughing up opposing ballcarriers for 11 seasons. **X**

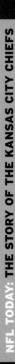
MEET THE CHIEFS

LEN DAWSON

QUARTERBACK
TEXANS/CHIEFS SEASONS: 1962-75
HEIGHT: 6 FEET
WEIGHT: 190 POUNDS

Len Dawson was exactly what coach Hank Stram needed to complete his championship-team assembly. Perhaps more importantly, Stram believed Dawson could lead the Chiefs for the long haul. Although Dawson was the top draft pick of the Pittsburgh Steelers in 1957, he floundered there and was traded to the Cleveland Browns. But Stram signed him in 1962 and let him fly. After starting only 2 games and throwing just 45 passes in his first 5 NFL seasons, Dawson had a positive and immediate effect on the Texans/Chiefs. He led the team to an AFL championship in his first season and earned the nickname "Lenny the Cool" with his calm, composed in-game demeanor and reserved personality off the field. "He was the quiet assassin," running back Ed Podolak said. "He could say more with a stare than most players could with words. He was the team leader, no doubt about it." While Dawson compiled impressive passing statistics, it never was about the numbers for this field general, because he focused completely on winning. "Lenny was our man," receiver Otis Taylor said. "He was our leader."

5-foot-10 and 184 pounds, Delaney was small in stature. But he made up for it with quick feet and a big heart, and he galloped 1,121 yards to earn AFC Rookie of the Year honors. With a stout defense led by ballhawking safety Gary Barbaro, the Chiefs improved to 9–7.

Then, after a strike-shortened 1982 season, tragedy struck on June 29, 1983. In an act of heroism, Delaney died while trying to save three boys from drowning near his home in Monroe, Louisiana. His teammates took the young star's passing hard. "Everyone knew he was a great football player," guard Tom Condon said. "But that was only a small part of what made him so special to us. As a young rookie, he played with cracked ribs, a broken wrist, a sprained knee. Then he had the courage to come back in his second year after detached retinas in both of his eyes, knowing there was a chance he could lose his sight. When those little kids needed help, he gave up his life trying to save them. He wasn't a swimmer.... The man had a tremendous heart—he was special."

After Delaney's death, the 1983 Chiefs slipped to 6–10, and Levy was fired. New coach John Mackovic took over and, by 1986, rebuilt the team into a surprise contender, largely through special-teams play. With 11 blocked kicks and 6 return touchdowns (off blocks and punt and kickoff returns), special

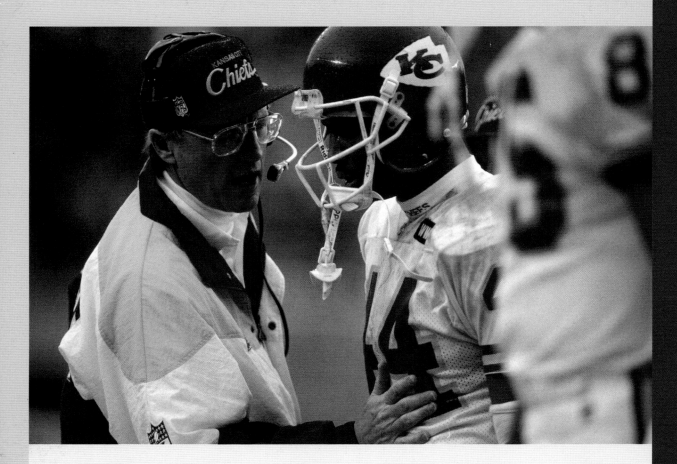

X Before arriving in Kansas City, coach Marty Schottenheimer had led the Cleveland Browns to the AFC Championship Game in both 1986 and 1987.

teams helped the Chiefs make the postseason for the first time in 15 years. But it was in and out, as they lost to the Jets 35–15.

Frustrated, Hunt shook up the franchise in December 1988. His first move was to hire general manager Carl Peterson, who had previously guided the Philadelphia Eagles, and give him complete control of the team's operations. Peterson moved quickly to name former Cleveland Browns head coach Marty Schottenheimer as the team's new sideline leader. "I believe the opportunity is there with this football team to once again approach that great tradition of the Kansas City Chiefs," said Schottenheimer. "My principal reason for selecting this opportunity is that I believe we can win—and win very, very quickly."

KANSAS CITY'S MR. MUSIC

Tony "Mr. Music" DiPardo was an established Kansas City orchestra leader when Lamar Hunt called him in 1963 and asked him to lead his stadium pep band. DiPardo agreed and has been with the Chiefs ever since. He started with the Zing Band in the city's old Municipal Stadium and moved along with the team into Arrowhead Stadium when it opened a decade later. There, he led the TD Pack Band from the southeastern end zone, rallying the faithful fans with live music. He even wrote fan-favorite songs about the Chiefs, including "The Chiefs Are on the Warpath" and "The Hank Stram Polka." In a fitting tribute, DiPardo performed "Taps" on his red-lacquered trumpet at the Chiefs' final home game in 2006 in recognition of Hunt's passing. He was considered so important to the club that Stram made sure he received a Super Bowl IV ring more than 30 years after the game. Former star kick returner Dante Hall also used to flip him the ball after scoring a touchdown. "Not bad," DiPardo said, "for a poor little Italian boy from St. Louis."

X Running back Christian Okoye's Chiefs career was short (six seasons) but memorable, marked by big on-field collisions and two Pro Bowls.

Schottenheimer installed "Marty Ball," an offense that featured Christian Okoye, a gigantic (6-foot-2 and 260 pounds) running back nicknamed "The Nigerian Nightmare." Okoye would lead the team in rushing for four seasons, including a club-record 1,480-yard effort in 1989. That year also saw the development of young defensive talent, including outstanding end Neil Smith and aggressive linebacker Derrick Thomas. This ferocious duo anchored a defense that emerged as one of the NFL's best.

A fierce pass rusher, Neil Smith hit the pinnacle of his career in 1993, making an NFL-leading 15 sacks and forcing 4 fumbles. **X**

HAIL TO THE CHIEFS

X- -

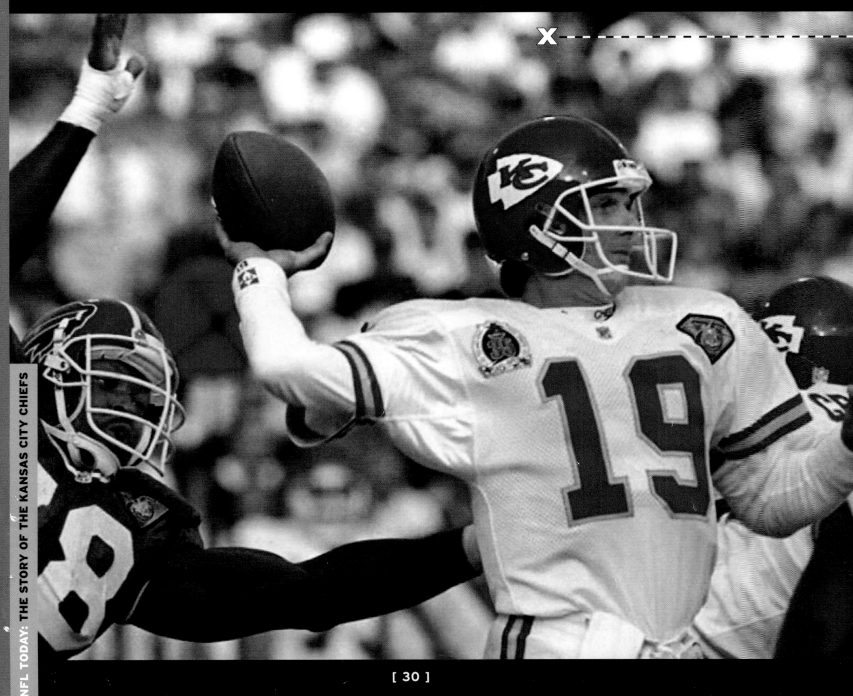

Kansas City earned its first playoff victory in 22 years by

beating the Los Angeles Raiders 10–6 in the 1991 playoffs.

Running back Barry Word pummeled the Raiders with a

Chiefs postseason-record 130 rushing yards, and the defense

stripped away 6 turnovers. Although the Chiefs lost to the

Buffalo Bills in the next round, Schottenheimer had his team

believing that greatness was possible. "The best way to

establish a position of excellence in the NFL," he explained,

"is to expect it."

After Kansas City was shut out in a 1992 playoff game

against the San Diego Chargers, Schottenheimer decided his

lineup needed some veteran leadership. The Chiefs made two

bold moves, trading for San Francisco 49ers quarterback Joe

Montana and signing running back Marcus Allen away from

the Raiders. While both stars were on the downside of their

legendary careers, they were revitalized with the fresh start

and led the Chiefs to the AFC West title in 1993. Allen scored a

league-high 12 rushing touchdowns to go along with 3 receiving

touchdowns and 1,002 total yards.

Montana, meanwhile, added an Arrowhead chapter to his

history of clutch performances in a 1993 playoff game against

the Steelers. After finding little offensive success in the first

three quarters, Montana led two fourth-quarter scoring

JAN STENERUD

KICKER
CHIEFS SEASONS: 1967-79
HEIGHT: 6-FOOT-2
WEIGHT: 187 POUNDS

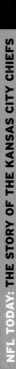

Who would ever have thought that a college basketball coach and a skier would alter the course of football kicking forever? Jan Stenerud attended Montana State University in the early 1960s on a skiing scholarship. During his sophomore year, he was spotted by the college's basketball coach booming footballs "soccer style," or from the side. Football coach Jim Sweeney was contacted immediately. "[Sweeney] saw me a couple of weeks later running the stadium steps," Stenerud recalls, "and he hollered at me, 'Hey, get down here. I hear you can kick.' So I kicked a few in front of the team. And they thought I had a chance, and they decided I should go out for spring practice." Stenerud starred for the next two years, during which he once kicked a then collegiate-record 59-yard field goal. Stenerud wasn't pro football's first soccer-style kicker, but he was arguably the best. He also never missed a game. At the time of his retirement, he ranked behind only George Blanda in all-time NFL scoring and later became the first pure placekicker elected to the Hall of Fame.

drives. The first, an efficient 9-play, 80-yard drive, resulted
in a 2-yard Allen touchdown run to tie the game 17–17. After
Kansas City fell behind again, Montana threw a fourth-down
touchdown to receiver Tim Barnett with less than two minutes
left in the game. Then, after missing an earlier field goal that
would have won the game, Chiefs kicker Nick Lowery went
from scapegoat to hero by booting the game-winner through
the uprights in overtime.

The Chiefs beat the Houston Oilers a week later, but their
luck ran out in Buffalo in their first-ever AFC Championship

X Although
receiver Tim Barnett
(left) played just three
NFL seasons, he was
pivotal in helping the
Chiefs reach their first
conference title game
in 1993.

Game. In the second quarter, Montana threw an end-zone strike to do-it-all running back Kimble Anders, but the ball popped out of Anders's hands and into those of Bills safety Henry Jones. In the third quarter, the vicious Buffalo defense knocked Montana out of the game with a concussion, and the Bills pulled away to win 30–13.

The Chiefs earned a playoff matchup against Miami in 1994 in what was a classic showcase for two of the game's best quarterbacks—Montana and Dan Marino. Each field general led his team to points on each first possession, and the game was tied 17–17 by halftime. Marino came out hot and broke the tie in the third quarter. Unfortunately, Kansas City's next pair of opportunities both ended in turnovers as the Dolphins won 27–17. Montana's career ended with this final loss.

Undaunted, the Chiefs reloaded in 1995 and compiled an NFL-best 13–3 record behind journeyman quarterback Steve Bono. In a home playoff game against a scrappy Indianapolis Colts team, Bono connected with wide receiver Lake Dawson for a long touchdown in the first quarter. But Kansas City's scoring ended there, as kicker Lin Elliott missed three field goals and the offense turned the ball over four times in a heartbreaking 10–7 loss. The playoffs were proving to be a

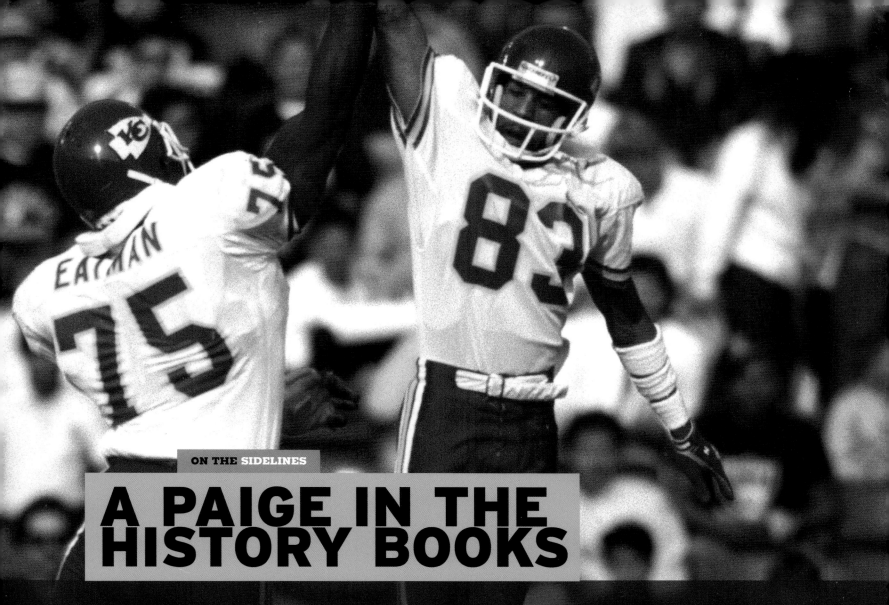

A PAIGE IN THE HISTORY BOOKS

During his nine-season stay in Kansas City, receiver Stephone Paige was considered a third-down player, but he never lost confidence in his abilities. "If I can make plays on third down," Paige wondered, "why can't I make them on first down? It's time to turn me loose." In the 1985 season finale against the San Diego Chargers, Paige was turned loose. And in the process, he broke Cleveland Rams receiver Jim Benton's 40-year-old NFL single-game receiving record of 303 yards. The plucky Paige went over 100 yards in the first quarter on just 2 catches. He had amassed 258 yards by the second quarter, which broke the Chiefs' single-game receiving record—in the first half! Paige hurt his ribs in the second quarter but returned late in the third to grab a 39-yard pass. Then, with about 5 minutes left in the game, Paige caught a 12-yarder that broke the record by 6 yards—309 total. Chiefs quarterback Bill Kenney admitted later he was determined to help Paige hit the mark "if I had to throw the ball to him five straight times."

DERRICK THOMAS

LINEBACKER
CHIEFS SEASONS: 1989-99
HEIGHT: 6-FOOT-3
WEIGHT: 243 POUNDS

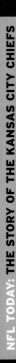

Derrick Thomas's contributions to the Chiefs were almost beyond measure. More than any other player, he changed the face and fortunes of the franchise when the Chiefs most needed it. "Derrick was the living embodiment of that Arrowhead Stadium noise," *Sports Illustrated* writer Michael Silver said. "It just seemed like he got his pass rush started a second earlier than the ball was snapped." Known for his "sack and strip" move, which caused many a fumble, Thomas was a devastating pass rusher who earned Defensive Rookie of the Year honors in 1989. But it was all a prelude to his sensational sophomore season, when he set a team record with 20 sacks, including an NFL-record 7 sacks in 1 game versus the Seattle Seahawks. In the 11 years that Thomas anchored the defense, the Chiefs finished first or second in the AFC West 10 times, made 7 playoff appearances, and won 3 division titles. Tragically, Thomas's career was cut short in 1999 when he died after a heart attack as a result of injuries suffered in a car accident. His number 58 jersey was never retired, but no one has worn it since.

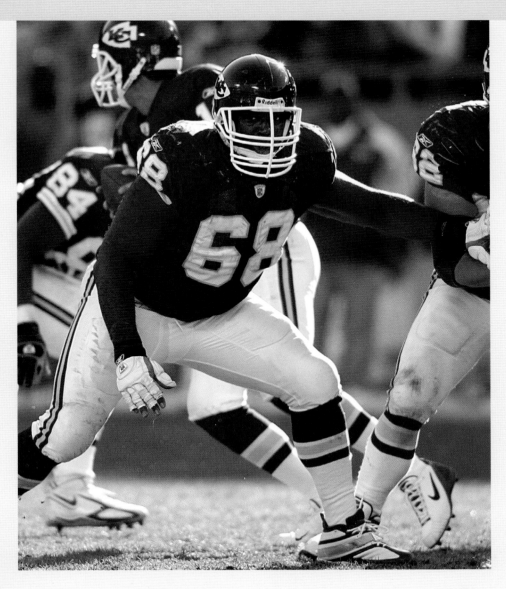

difficult and frustrating obstacle for Coach Schottenheimer.

After having made the playoffs every year from 1990 to 1995, the Chiefs did so once more in 1997 with the help of such players as rookie tight end Tony Gonzalez, quarterback Elvis Grbac, receiver Andre Rison, and guard Will Shields. But after losing 14–10 to the Denver Broncos in the postseason, the Chiefs slipped from atop the AFC West. After his team dropped to 7–9 in 1998, Schottenheimer resigned.

X Star guard Will Shields never missed a game in his 14-year Chiefs career, starting an incredible 230 straight contests.

X Linebacker
Derrick Thomas had
a knack for getting
to the ball and then
ripping it loose, forcing
an NFL-record 45
fumbles in his career.

CHANGING WITH
THE MILLENNIUM

During head coach Gunther Cunningham's two years, Kansas City went 9–7 in 1999 and 7–9 in 2000. But there were signs of a Chiefs turnaround in 2001 when Peterson finally got the coach he had always wanted—Dick Vermeil, who had previously coached the cross-state St. Louis Rams to a 1999 Super Bowl victory. "Twelve years ago, Lamar Hunt and his family gave me an opportunity to run this franchise," Peterson said at the press conference announcing the hiring. "And at that time, there was only one man on my mind I would like to be the head coach of the Kansas City Chiefs."

Expectations ran high when Vermeil brought in Rams backup quarterback Trent Green and Baltimore Ravens running back Priest Holmes. Holmes had the finest season of his career in 2002 behind tackle Willie Roaf and guard Brian Waters, the dominant left side on one of the league's best offensive lines. A dual running and receiving threat, Holmes broke loose for an AFC-best 2,287 total yards and 24 touchdowns and led the team with 70 receptions. "He is doing stuff that has never been done in the history of the NFL, especially with those touchdowns," Gonzalez said of the electrifying halfback.

Dangerous kick returner Dante Hall also broke out that

X Halfback Priest Holmes won a Super Bowl XXXV ring with the Ravens in 2000 but didn't become a star with his powerful, high-stepping style until suiting up for the Chiefs in 2001.

year with a punt and two kickoffs returned for touchdowns. His game-changing, open-field running kept opponents nervous and earned him a Pro Bowl selection. "It's just an unbelievable feeling," Hall said. "I never could have seen anything like this happen, going from struggling to make the team to going to the Pro Bowl." Yet despite all of the individual success, the Chiefs ended the season 8–8.

In 2003, the offense was even better, scoring a club-record 484 points as Holmes rolled up an NFL-record 27 touchdowns. Safety Jerome Woods headed up a defensive unit that led the league in turnover ratio. Hall also improved, scoring touchdowns on two punts and two kickoff returns. The high-powered Chiefs went 13–3 to easily win the AFC West.

At home in Arrowhead for the playoffs, the Chiefs squared off against the Colts in what turned out to be the first punt-free game in NFL playoff history. Although Holmes shattered the Chiefs' single-game postseason rushing record with 176 yards and 2 touchdowns, he fumbled away the game's only turnover. Coach Vermeil's decision to not try an onside kick late in the fourth quarter sealed the Chiefs' fate with a 38–31 loss.

After Holmes was injured during a 7–9 season in 2004, powerful young halfback Larry Johnson picked up the

ON THE SIDELINES

BLOOD RIVALS

The Kansas City Chiefs and Oakland Raiders share one of sports' oldest and nastiest rivalries—a rivalry that dates back to the days of the AFL. But it took a decidedly familial turn in 1995 with the Cash brothers. Keith (Chiefs) and Kerry (Raiders) Cash, identical-twin tight ends, spent the majority of their lives playing on the same team. So neither player could have imagined being thrust onto opposite sides of one of the NFL's most heated battles. Despite the bitter relationship of their employers, the brothers' bond remained intact, if not a little different. For one thing, each brother had to stop hoping the other would win. While watching a Raiders game on Monday Night Football, Keith remembered, "I wanted him to play well—but I also wanted his team to lose." It even affected their mother, Sarah. Because she was conflicted, she bought a custom-made jacket—with a Chiefs logo on the front and a Raiders logo on the back. "She was the only one in the stadium who wanted a tie," said Keith, who played five seasons with the Chiefs. "Actually, it was easy for her. All she had to do was cheer for the offense."

ON THE SIDELINES

THE BATTLE TO BRAG

The Governor's Cup trophy has been a staple of Missouri pro football for more than 40 years. The preseason—and sometimes regular-season—contest between the Chiefs and their intrastate rivals, the St. Louis Rams, has been referred to as "The Battle of Missouri" or "I-70 Series." The tradition started in 1968 against the St. Louis Cardinals. When the Cardinals moved to Arizona in 1987, the Chiefs held a dominant 16–7–2 advantage in the rivalry. The series resumed in 1995 when the Los Angeles Rams relocated to St. Louis. It took on new meaning in 2001 when the Chiefs hired former Rams coach Dick Vermeil. After molding the Rams into one of the most powerful offensive squads in NFL history and winning Super Bowl XXXIV, Vermeil installed the same offense in Kansas City. In the early 2000s, the teams boasted two of the most productive offenses in the NFL, and what used to be a sometimes-meaningless game became a high-energy shootout for state bragging rights. While the Chiefs were 6–4 in the preseason against the Rams (by 2008), they were 4–0 in the all-important regular season.

rushing load. Then, after the Chiefs missed the playoffs again in 2005, Vermeil retired. In 2006, new coach Herm Edwards focused his offense on Johnson, and the workhorse back responded with an NFL-record 416 rushing attempts that helped carry the Chiefs back into the postseason. But in a first-round matchup against Indianapolis, the Chiefs' offense fizzled in a lopsided 23–8 loss.

After Kansas City plummeted to 4–12 in 2007, finishing the season with nine straight losses, Roaf retired. The

X Carrying the ball more times than any NFL rusher ever had in a season, Larry Johnson charged for a franchise-record 1,789 yards in 2006.

TONY GONZALEZ

TIGHT END
CHIEFS SEASONS: 1997–2008
HEIGHT: 6-FOOT-5
WEIGHT: 251 POUNDS

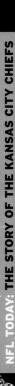

Calling an active NFL player a "future Hall-of-Famer" is often considered either a jinx or undeserved credit. But Tony Gonzalez will probably finish his career with more catches, yards, and touchdowns than any other tight end in pro football history. Yet statistics weren't everything to Gonzalez, who said, "I want to be a complete football player for this team." Gonzalez became an excellent blocker, and it made him one of the most well-rounded tight ends in the game. While most of the game's best tight ends excel at racking up receiving statistics, few are considered great blockers. During one 2004 game in which the Chiefs ran for 8 touchdowns, Gonzalez caught only 2 passes for 19 yards. But the commanding rushing performance was due, in large part, to Gonzalez's blocking, and because of that, his teammates and coaches considered it one of his best games ever. "I think he just got tired of people making fun of his blocking [early in his career]," Chiefs guard Brian Waters said. "Because, man, he was just crushing people. He just fights and fights."

Chiefs also began building for the future by trading away one of their brightest stars, pass-rushing defensive end Jared Allen, for extra picks in the 2008 NFL Draft. "Herm [Edwards] has been consistent in how he wants to build a football team, and that's what we're doing," Peterson explained. The team used its top pick on big defensive tackle Glenn Dorsey, who was added to a defensive line that already featured up-and-coming pass rusher Tamba Hali. Although the Chiefs remained stuck at the bottom of their division in 2008, the Kansas City faithful hoped that these players—along with young wide receiver Dwayne Bowe—would soon turn things around.

For more than four decades, fans in Kansas City have cheered for their Chiefs. With a resumé that includes an appearance in the very first Super Bowl, a Super Bowl IV victory, and six consecutive playoff berths in the 1990s, the Chiefs have often been counted among the NFL's elite. Now, as they continue down the warpath, they intend to bring another NFL championship to western Missouri very soon.

INDEX